SUPERHERO

Dedicated to Janne

GAZELLE

Dad says I run like a gazelle...
That's because there's one inside of me.
All through the night in my dreams...
The gazelle and I explore her home territory.

She introduces me to the other gazelles...
We speak gazelle as we stand and share water.
Her Bovidae family makes me feel welcome...
Her buck and doe parents are proud of their
daughter!

When morning comes and it's time for school...
The gazelle and I run all the way!
With the help of the speedy fawn inside of me...
We hope to win a gold medal one day!

FOX

I've heard about foxes who are clever...
But not about foxes who are shy.
The fox living inside of me asks me lots of questions...
Such as: "Why am I so shy?"

"Why do we need to go outside?" he asks.
"And why do the birds always sing?
"Why does everyone think foxes are clever?
When I am shy about every single thing?"

I reply, "Outside is where the sky is blue.
"And where the grass is greener than green.
"It's where the trees and flowers live...
"Where beauty exists in every scene."

"As to the birds," I continue...
"The language they speak is in song.
"It's how they communicate with each other...
"Talking and sharing can't be wrong."

The fox inside of me waits patiently...
Soon I add, "Foxes are clever, it's in your DNA!
"It has been coded in your genetics...
"So come on, let's go out and play!"

LAMB

I live in an apartment in the city...
City life hasn't done me any harm.
Still somedays a part of me wishes...
I'd been born in the country on a farm.

One morning I woke up and all I could say was,
"BAAAAAAAA!"
Dad asked, "Why are you being such a ham?"
I grabbed my laptop and typed in...
"I think I've been invaded by a lamb!"

Dad sniggered, it's what nervous people do...
While the lamb inside of me bleated.
Like a crazy lamb I ran around my room...
Until my lamb's wool became overheated.

Dad left and brought back a bottle of water...
I sipped it until I cooled down again.
I thanked him by bleating another, "BAAAAAA!"
Dad couldn't help it, he sniggered again.

When I woke up the very next morning...
The lamb inside of me had gone.
Dad surprised me with a pair of lamb's wool boots...
But I'm too scared to put them on!

PUPPY

I sat on the floor among all my toys...
Then crossed my arms not knowing what to do.
It seems I had forgotten how to play...
A voice inside said, "I'm a puppy and I can help you!"

And just like that a labrador puppy inside of me was born...
Boy did he know how to play!
I taught him how to share my things...
And he taught me how to play the puppy way!

On my Fifth Birthday morning...
The labrador puppy living inside of me...
Came to life: a furry ball in my arms.
He still is the best birthday present ever given to me!

EAGLE

I'm tired of walking and running everywhere!
The eagle inside of me wants us to fly!
To rise up and soar above the earth together!
Where I can see the world through his eagle-eyes.

To dive down from high up and catch a fish...
To share our captured feast.
Then sit upon a mountain and observe...
As the sun breathes a new day in the east.

And after a full day of flying and exploring...
When I go to bed, I dream I see...
A new adventure ahead...
With the eagle inside of me.

REWIND

Did you ever wish you could change something?
A memory or thought to be left behind?
On some days, I wish I could do that...
I wish I could HIT REWIND.

So, I decided to invent a button...
A button Inside of me.
When I remember something I want to forget...
Something sad, scary, or hurtful to me.

I'm not trying to change the past!
But I like having the power to, in my mind.
To change my own perspective...
All I have to do is HIT REWIND.

It's like I have built a new window for myself...
If something happens, if someone is unkind...
In my imagination I push the button...
And it's easy to reset my mind.

My brain is a powerful tool...
My own personal computer by design...
It gives me power when...
All I have to do is HIT REWIND.

TWIST

Last night when I was sleepwalking...
I woke up in a twist!
My head was banging...
I think you get the gist!

My sister came running out of her room!
She asked, "Why are you in a twist?"
I didn't know what I was doing so...
She said, "What you look like, is THIS!"

Between us we made quite a racket!
Dad and mom came out to see!
"What the heck is going on?" they asked.
Awake now I said, "There's a twist inside of me!

Next thing I know they were all a-twist too...
We were banging our heads crazily!
At least I had an excuse...
Since there was a twist inside of me!

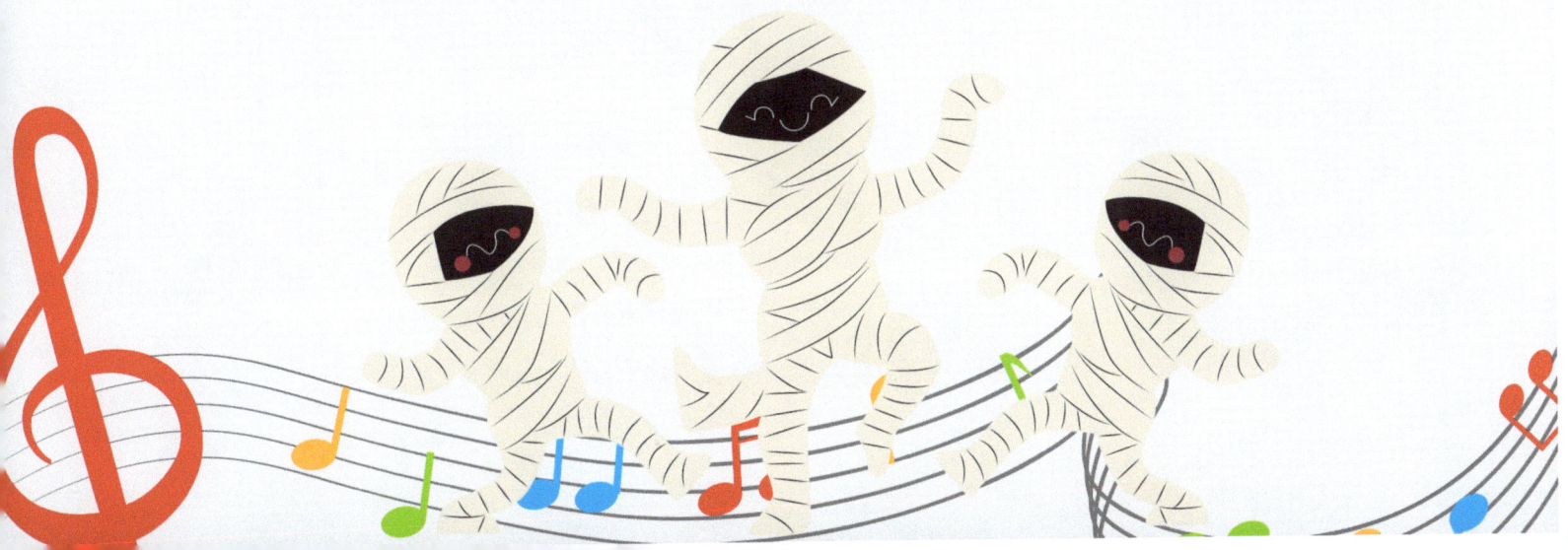

TORNADO

Sometimes when I get ANGRY...
There's a tornado inside of me!
If I don't let it out, I'll explode!
I'm afraid I'll harm someone I love
dearly.

"Take a few deep breaths,"
Advises the tornado inside of me.
"Think about calm things, like the
sky.
"Then you won't need to be afraid
of me!"

The tornado inside, calmed me down...
And now I meditate quietly every night.
There is still a tornado living inside of me...
Together we'll both be all right!

PARK

Since I fell and broke my leg the other day...
There's been a park living inside of me.
In that park, I climb, swing and play...
But it's only imaginary.

When the doctor removes the cast from my leg...
It'll be back to the real park for me!
Until then I'll keep safe by playing...
In the imaginary park inside of me!

MERMAID

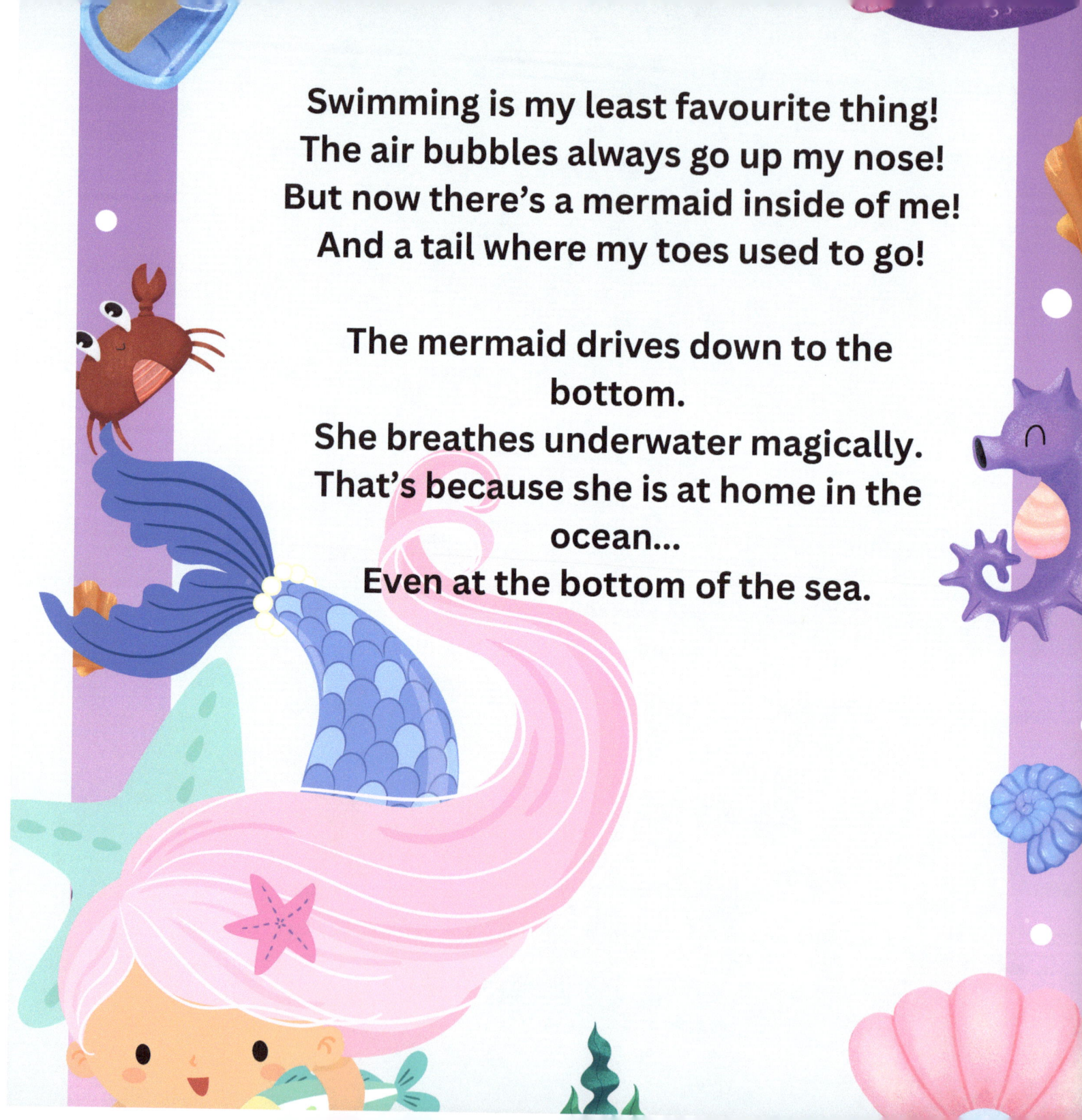

Swimming is my least favourite thing!
The air bubbles always go up my nose!
But now there's a mermaid inside of me!
And a tail where my toes used to go!

The mermaid drives down to the bottom.
She breathes underwater magically.
That's because she is at home in the ocean...
Even at the bottom of the sea.

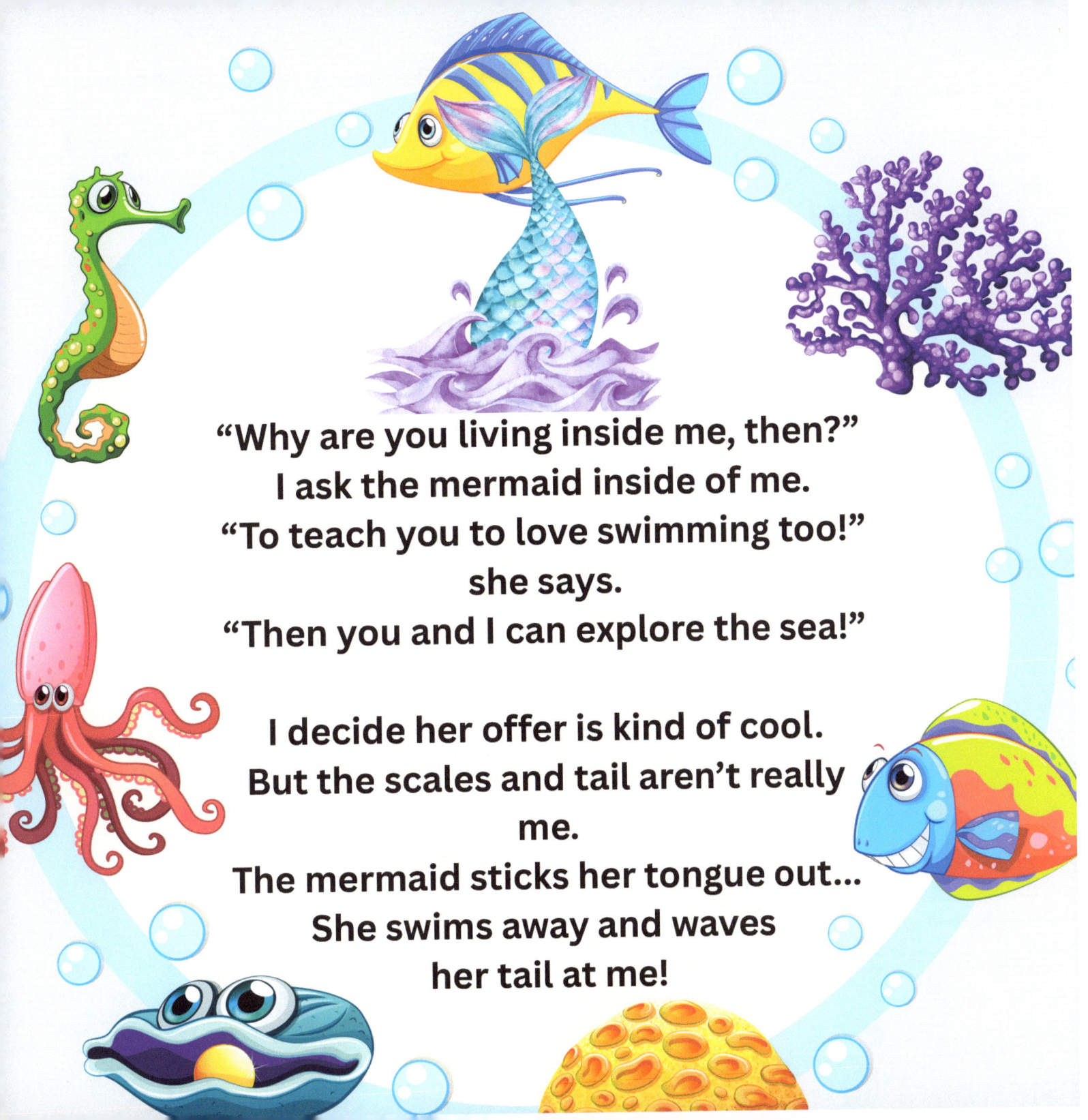

"Why are you living inside me, then?"
I ask the mermaid inside of me.
"To teach you to love swimming too!"
she says.
"Then you and I can explore the sea!"

I decide her offer is kind of cool.
But the scales and tail aren't really
me.
The mermaid sticks her tongue out...
She swims away and waves
her tail at me!

CUCKOO

Weird things keep happening!
Since a cuckoo took up inside of me!
Mom asked, "Aren't cuckoos extinct?"
I decided to check for myself and see.

Ends up most have been extinct...
But the one inside of me.
Says he intends to stick around...
He tells the time every hour, 1 a.m., 2 a.m., 3!

I was so very happy when Daylight Savings began...
Because it confused the cuckoo in me.
He kept popping his head out at the wrong time...
And waking up everybody!

MACHINE

When I'm being tested at school...
There's a machine inside of me.
It shuffles and stores the information I've been taught...
And makes it a part of me.

When I sleep, I dream...
Of the machine inside of me.
Through making sense of all I've learned...
While it is storing it all in my memory.

When it comes time to take the test...
I PASS! And the teacher gives me an A.
With the help of the computer inside of me...
We hope to achieve an A+ some day!

PORPOISE

The porpoise has a purpose...
I have one living inside of me.
I don't know the porpoise's purpose...
The purpose of the porpoise perplexes me!

PARROT

I repeat the things people say...
There's a parrot inside of me.
She gets me into all kinds of trouble...
And sometimes makes me dizzy!

Dizzy, when people I hear spin and talk...
Because to parrot, I need to spin too!
Which makes my tummy feel funny!
Especially when I parrot someone new!

Then I discovered an interesting trick...
Some say it is rude...Perhaps you'll agree?
When I want a day off from parroting...
I MUTE the parrot inside of me!

POEM

Writing a poem can be such fun!
When I write, each poem is alive in me.
I sound out the words and the rhymes...
And let inspiration take over me!

I love the challenge of a blank page...
Waiting for an idea to come to me.
Poems always come from the heart...
Poetry can be serious, or funny!

If you haven't yet tried to write a poem...
I highly recommend that you do.
You might even begin a new adventure...
And find there's a poet living inside of you, too!

Sitting in a wheelchair near a hill looking down...
There's a whisper inside of me.
It says, "Wouldn't your friends be surprised...
"If you went down there yourself to see?"

The hill wasn't really a hill...
It was a mound...I could steer down easily.
But my friends had said I should stay put...
As they'd be coming back for me.

The whisper inside me whispered again...
"But up here, you're missing all the fun!"
I could hear them laughing and playing down there...
Had I been forgotten by everyone?

I didn't think so...but I still went down...
I smiled when my friends saw me.
"Next time you won't underestimate yourself!" the whisper whispered...
As my friends threw their arms around me.

RAVEN

A raven sits outside my window...
Her raven sister lives inside of me.
She sings, "It's time to explore the night!
"Come out! Come out and see!"

I glance at the clock and it's midnight...
Her sister ruffles her feathers in me.
While the sister raven sings outside...
From high up in a dark, dark tree.

I climb out very carefully onto
the branch...
We sit side by side, the sister
ravens and me.
We sing until the sun comes up...
Then I set the raven inside me
free.

HERO

I'm too shy to be a hero.
And I'm afraid of heights too!
But what else can you do?
When there's a hero living inside of you?

The other day a neighbour's kitten...
Was stuck up in a tree.
There was no one around to rescue her...
Except for the hero in me.

I ran and asked Dad if I could borrow the ladder.
He said yes, so I secured it against the tree.
My knees knocked and trembled...
Still I climbed up, and rescued the kitty.

Later the firetrucks arrived...
The firefighters said they were impressed with me.
They gave me a round of applause...
I'm hero of the day - that's me!

BRIDGE

I crossed above the free-flowing waters...
Using the bridge inside of me.
It all happened inside my mind...
Where I travelled to Australia - Sydney!

Bridges are so cool and inspiring!
I hope to design one of my own one day.
Perhaps on Mars, Jupiter, or the Moon...
Where there's a will - there's a way!

TWINS

I prefer dogs to cats...
Or I did briefly...
Until twin cats...
Started living inside of me.

When they spoke in cat talk...
I didn't understand their cat chattery.
Which was totally fine....
Because they couldn't understand me!

MY POEM

_____

_____

_____

_____

_____

_____

_____

_____

_____

_____

MY POEM OR DRAWING

ALSO BY CATHY MCGOUGH

POETRY SERIES:

There's a Chimpanzee Inside of Me!
There's a Jumping Bean Inside of Me!
There's a Reindeer Inside of Me!

JUMP SERIES:

Jump Like a Caribou!
Jump Like a Kangaroo!
Jump at the Zoo!
Jump and Say P.U.!
Jump and Say Boo!
Jump and Say Valentine's Day Is
For Kids Too!
Jump and Look For a Clue!
Jump and Say Happy Birthday to You!
Jump For Everything Blue!
Jump, Hop and Say Happy Easter To You!
Jump and Say Cock-A-Doodle-Do!
Jump and Sing Da-Do-Do-Do!
Jump and Ask Who? Who?
Jump and Squawk Like a Cockatoo!
Jump and Ask Is It You or Ewe?
Jump and Say There's an Ewww in My Stew!
Jump and Say Merry Christmas To You!
Jump and Cheer Happy New Year!
Jump and Say There's a Moo-Moo in a Tutu!
Jump and Say There's a Hare in My Hair!
Jump and Say My Aunt Ate An Ant!
Jump and Say There's An Aardvark
In The Amusement Park!
Jump and Roar For The Dinosaurs!
Jump and Buzz Like A Bee!
Jump and Flutter Like A Butterfly!
Jump and Pop Like Popcorn!
Jump and Ribbit Like A Frog!
Jump and Snore Like A Koala!

Jump and Snuffle Like A Platypus!
Jump and Grunt Like A Groundhog!
Jump and Say Hello!
Jump and Say Friend!
Jump and Say Peace!
Jump and Say Sky!
Jump and Say Merry Christmas!
Jump and Say Happy New Year!
Jump and Say Fun!
Jump and Say Family!
Jump and Say Jump!

CLAP FOR SERIES:

Clap for 1!
Clap for 2!
Clap for 3!
Clap for 4!
Clap for 5!
Clap for 6!
Clap for 7!
Clap for 8!
Clap for 9!
Clap for 10!

The Cat Who Said Hello
The Three Boulders
Billy Shakespeare
Billie Shakespeare
Learn To Draw With Symmetry
ABC More Learn to Draw With Symmetry

Non-Fiction
103 Fundraising Ideas For Parent Volunteers With Schools and Teams